# THE LITTLE BOOK OF

# TEA TIPS



ANDREW LANGLEY

# THE LITTLE BOOK OF

# TEA TIPS

ANDREW LANGLEY

Absolute Press

First published in Great Britain in 2005 by
**Absolute Press**
Scarborough House, 29 James Street West
Bath BA1 2BT, England
**Phone** 44 (0) 1225 316013 **Fax** 44 (0) 1225 445836
**E-mail** info@absolutepress.co.uk
**Web** www.absolutepress.co.uk

Reprinted 2007.



A catalogue record of this book is available from the British Library

**ISBN 13: 9781904573326**

Printed and bound in China by 1010 International

'Tea-leaves should have folds like
the leather boots of tartar horsemen and
curls like the dewlaps of a mighty ox;
they should be moist and soft to the
touch, like the earth freshly swept by rain.'

**Lu-yu**
*Chinese poet*

# 1

**For a delicious** and unusual **ice cream flavouring,** soak prunes overnight in orange juice, Armagnac, and an Earl Grey tea bag covered with boiling water. Next day strain the liquid, add sugar and reduce it to a syrup. Mix with fromage blanc and freeze.

# 2

Large leafed tea needs **a longer brewing time.**

The hot water takes longer to extract the contents from the bigger surface area.

# 3

Home-made rice tea is

# a traditional Chinese delicacy.

And it's easy to brew.

Gently toast 2 tablespoons of rice in a frying pan until dark and nicely aromatic. Then simmer in a pan with 1 litre of water for a minute. Steep for a while, then strain and drink.

# 4

# Brew your own health-giving ginger tea.

Peel and chop a finger-length piece of ginger root and put in a pan with about 2 litres of water. Boil covered for 25 minutes, then uncovered for a further 15 minutes. Strain and drink.

# 5

**Green tea and apples** go together perfectly. Brew and strain a pot of green tea, then leave it to cool. Then add a slug of apple juice and pieces of freshly-sliced eating apple.

# 6

**Roast chicken** can be **given a gentle lift** by tea leaves.

Put a sheet of foil on the bottom of the roasting tin, sprinkle with tea leaves and sugar, and put the chicken on top. Roast in the normal way until the chicken skin is brown and crispy.

# 7

Ordinary iced tea is one thing, but

# spicy icy tea

is quite another. Brew up an aromatic tea such as Earl Grey, strain into a jug and add the following – cardamom pods, coriander seeds and black peppercorns (all crushed). Leave to steep for 3 hours, and mix in honey to taste.

# 8

**Give a lift** to an ordinary cuppa by adding fresh mint. Pop 3 or 4 sprigs of mint into the pot with the tea leaves (preferably Chinese) and brew in the normal way.

# 9

# The first tea out of the pot is the weakest.

So start by pouring a little tea into each cup, then top them up. This way, each cup will be of equal strength.

# 10

**The best tea bread** actually contains tea. Soak 450g of dried fruit overnight in a cup of strong black tea and a cup of sugar. Next day stir in one cup of self-raising flour and a beaten egg, mixing thoroughly. Put in a greased loaf tin and bake for about one hour.

# 11

# The best water for brewing tea

is 'soft', or low in calcium. This brings out the taste and aroma most effectively. If you live in a 'hard' water area, look for a tea specially designed to cope with the extra calcium.

# 12

Get rid of **unwanted odours in the fridge,** using another of tea's amazing properties. Fill a cotton or muslin bag with green tea leaves and leave it inside the refrigerator.

# 13

# Yogi tea

was first developed in California during the Flower Power era of the 1960s. To make your own, **crush** cardamom seeds, black peppercorns, cloves, cinnamon stick and ginger root in a mortar. **Simmer** in water for 20 minutes, then **add a pinch** of black tea. **Pour** and add milk and honey to taste.

# 14

Many people like a slice of lemon in their tea, instead of milk. For a change,

# why not try a slice of orange?

It adds an intriguing new dimension to the taste.

# 15

**When brewing green tea,** use water at a lower temperature. It should not be boiling but between 65-70°C (150-175°F). This preserves the colour and health-giving properties of the tea.

# 16

# Always let green tea steep with the lid off.

This allows the liquid to cool off slightly quicker, so that it brews more gently.

# 17

# For the last word in Chinese tea-making,

you have to use the correct equipment. This means delicate Oolong tea leaves brewed in a special pot which is surrounded by an outer chamber. Hot water is poured in to keep the tea warm while it is steeping.

# 18

# Every tea pot needs a thorough clean occasionally

to get rid of tannin stains. Fill it up with very hot water and drop in a fizzy denture-cleaning tablet. Make sure you tip the pot to get the solution up the spout. Leave for at least one hour before rinsing.

# 19

# Making iced green tea is simple and quick

– and rather dramatic.

Make the tea twice as strong as normal, but so that it half fills a pyrex jug. After two minutes, add ice cubes until the liquid reaches the top. Strain into glasses over more ice.

# 20

Whenever possible,

# buy loose tea leaves rather than tea bags.

Loose leaves are open for inspection, but many brands of tea bag are filled with all sorts of tea dust and 'fanning' (fragments) of lower quality.

# 21

Tea is a valuable

# fertilizer for your garden.

It contains useful quantities of nitrogen, potash and other nutrients for plants. So always empty your tea pot onto the flower bed or the compost heap.

# 22

# Keep your tea in a metal tin

or dark glass jar, and not in the packet or bag you bought it in. Store out of direct sunlight or excessive heat, and it will last for a long time.

# 23

Brew your tea in a proper teapot.

**Tea leaves need space to expand** and release their flavours. They can't do this within the straitjacket of a spoon or ball infuser – or a tea bag.

# 24

**The best tea pot of all** is a cast iron one, which retains the heat for the best brewing. Cast iron is pricey, though. The preferable substitute is an earthenware pot – not one of glass or steel, which lose heat far too fast.

# 25

**Used tea bags** can be laid on the eyes to rest them and **smooth out wrinkles.** Some say that this is also an effective treatment for removing styes and other eye infections.

# 26

Timing is vital, so **use a timer at first when brewing.**

Delicate black teas need no more than 3 to 5 minutes, and green teas up to 7 minutes. After this, more tannins will be extracted from the leaves, spoiling the taste.

# 27

**For an intriguing variation on iced tea,** try making classic Chinese bubble tea. Put a tablespoon of cooked tapioca pearls in the bottom of a long glass. Blend a cup of strong black tea plus the same amount of ice in a cocktail shaker and pour over. Drink through a straw.

28

Hot Christmas tea is the **ideal winter warmer.**

Boil water in a saucepan, turn off the heat and add teabags, cinnamon stick and cloves. After it has brewed for five minutes, stir in sugar, cranberry juice and a glass of red wine. Serve hot with slices of orange or apple.

29

**Remove tea stains from upholstery** by washing as soon as possible with a biological detergent. Dab stubborn stains on white material with a very weak (10 to 1) solution of hydrogen peroxide in water.

# 30

If you own an ice cream maker,

# it's easy to make tea granita.

Simply brew up and strain off about I litre of tea and stir in sugar. When cool, put in to the ice cream maker and slowly add a cup of milk. When it looks creamy, add a glass of white rum, blend and freeze.

# 31

Here's something robustly different:

# East African chai.

Fill a pot halfway with water and boil. Add 3 tea bags and top up with milk (yes, really). Bring back to the boil, pour into mugs and drink with lots of sugar.

# 32

Everybody knows that you should

**warm the pot**

before brewing tea.

**But** it is just as important to **also warm the tea cups** as well. Fill with hot water, and empty just before pouring out the tea.

# 33

You may not have a samovar, but you can still make **Russian tea.** Brew up a strong pot of black tea and strain it into a saucepan. Add sugar, orange juice, pineapple juice, a little lemon juice and a few cloves, then simmer for 30 minutes.

# 34

**Tea makes an unusual marinade,** especially for chicken or vegetables. Try marinating some freshly-cooked French beans in a mixture of brewed tea (cooled) and chopped garlic.

# 35

**Iced tea** is usually served in glasses, so it **should be as clear as possible.** Water which is too alkaline can make the tea cloudy. If this is the case, put in slices of lemon or lime to add acid and help keep the brew clear.

# 36

Rooibos tea from South Africa is **ideal for drinkers trying to avoid caffeine.** It is caffeine-free, and is said to be good for hay fever and eczema. Rooibos can even be used (when cold) to calm skin rashes and other infections.

37

# Always make tea with freshly drawn water,

which is well mixed with oxygen. Oxygen is vital to bring out the taste and aroma, so never use standing water or even bottled water. For the same reason, use water as soon as it boils, before the oxygen is lost.

# 38

**Chicken pieces** taste wonderful if **braised in tea.** Brew and strain the tea, add sugar, tomato purée and chopped garlic and onions. Brown the chicken pieces in olive oil, then pour over the braising mixture and cook for about 40 minutes.

# 39

The Gongfu brewing method **brings out the very best in a fine black tea.** Place the tea leaves in a warm pot and fill with hot water. Immediately, strain off the water. This rinses the leaves, which are now ready for a second dose of hot water, and a short brewing time (no more than 3 minutes).

# 40

Lapsang Souchong or green tea leaves

**add a smokey flavour to baked firm white fish.** Roll the fish in the tea and a little salt and pepper, then wrap in foil. Bake for 15 to 20 minutes in a hot oven.

# 41

If you ever find

**the legendary Dragon Well Tea of China,**

try this amazing recipe. Brew the tea for 15 minutes. Stir-fry some peeled shrimps with rice wine in a wok. After 30 seconds pour in the tea. After another minute remove the shrimps, reduce the liquid by half and pour it over.

# 42

Always **keep** stored tea well **away from** garlic, spices and other **strong smelling foods.**

Their aromas can interfere with the tea's delicate oils and affect the taste.

# 43

**You can freeze tea.** Brew up a pot of your favourite, strain the liquid and then freeze it in cube trays. When you want a quick cuppa, simply take out five or six cubes and de-frost.

# 44

# Saffron tea has an extraordinary taste...

and a beautiful colour.

Soak 12 saffron threads in a little water until the water is coloured. Add 3 cups of water, 1 cup of milk and some cardamom seed. Boil for 5 minutes, pop in a couple of teabags and leave to stand before straining.

# 45

Tea leaves can make

**a subtle addition to soups and stews.** Crush a heaped table spoonful of green tea leaves on a board with a rolling pin, and pop into the pot about 20 minutes before serving.

# 46

**Always drink tea freshly brewed.** Once left to stand, it loses aroma, and the oxygen in the air changes its colour and taste.

# 47

# Marbling turns a humble egg into a work of art.

Hard-boil some eggs for 10 minutes. Remove them (keep the water) and gently crack the shells all over. Put 3 teabags into the water, plus a little salt. Return the eggs and simmer for 20 minutes. When cool, remove the shells and – hey presto!

48

The combination of

# peppermint tea and hot chocolate

is magical. Heat a cup of milk with a peppermint tea bag to just boiling. Turn off the heat, remove the tea bag and add a tablespoon of drinking chocolate. Stir energetically.

# 49

A green tea poultice has a

**soothing effect on nasty insect bites.** Brew the tea, then strain the leaves and squeeze out as much water as possible. Press the leaves on the bitten area of skin.

50

Milk in tea? Yes. A slice of lemon? Certainly.

# But never mix the two in the same cup.

The acid in the lemon juice will curdle the milk and leave it looking and tasting most peculiar.

Andrew Langley

Andrew Langley is a knowledgeable food and drink writer. Among his formative influences he lists a season picking grapes in Bordeaux, several years of raising sheep and chickens in Wiltshire and two decades drinking his grandmother's tea. He has written books on a number of Scottish and Irish whisky distilleries and is the editor of the highly regarded anthology of the writings of the legendary Victorian chef Alexis Soyer.

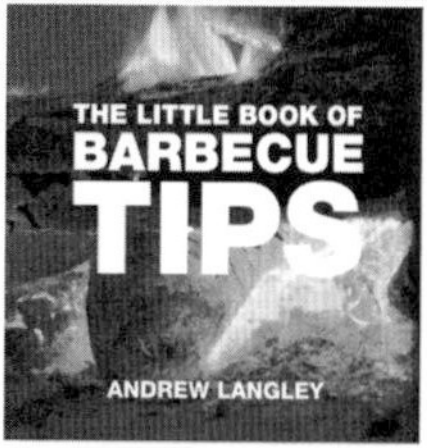
THE LITTLE BOOK OF
BARBECUE
TIPS
ANDREW LANGLEY

THE LITTLE BOOK OF
BEER
TIPS
ANDREW LANGLEY

THE LITTLE BOOK OF
HERB
TIPS
WILLIAM FORTT

THE LITTLE BOOK OF
POKER
TIPS
PETER FRENCH

THE LITTLE BOOK OF
GARDENING
TIPS
WILLIAM FORTT
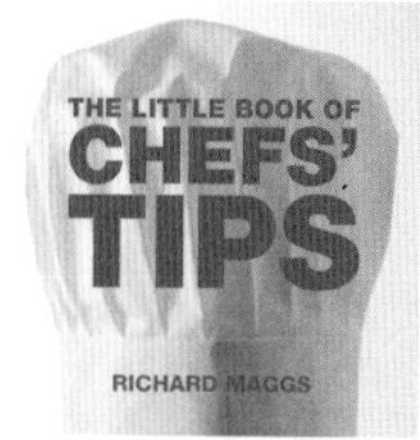
THE LITTLE BOOK OF
CHEFS'
TIPS
RICHARD MAGGS

THE LITTLE BOOK OF
SPICE
TIPS
ANDREW LANGLEY

THE LITTLE BOOK OF
GOLF
TIPS
PETER FRENCH

THE LITTLE BOOK OF
TIPS
SERIES

THE LITTLE BOOK OF
CHEESE
TIPS
ANDREW LANGLEY

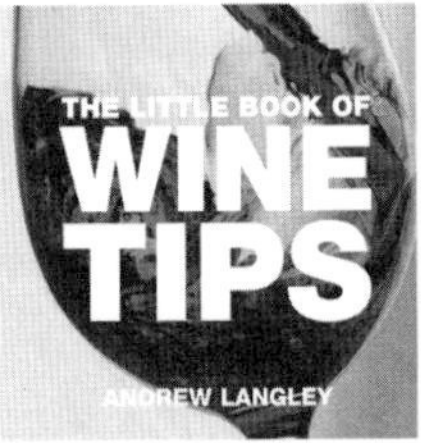
THE LITTLE BOOK OF
WINE
TIPS
ANDREW LANGLEY

THE LITTLE BOOK OF
AGA
TIPS²
RICHARD MAGGS

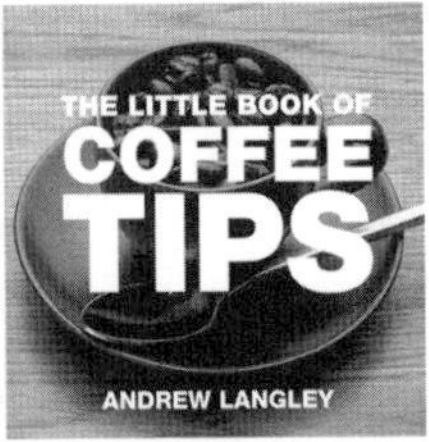
THE LITTLE BOOK OF
COFFEE
TIPS
ANDREW LANGLEY

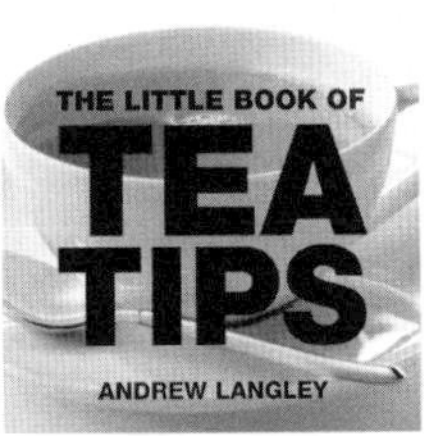
THE LITTLE BOOK OF
TEA
TIPS
ANDREW LANGLEY

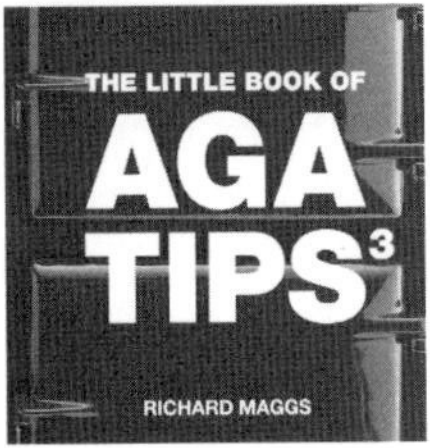
THE LITTLE BOOK OF
AGA
TIPS³
RICHARD MAGGS

THE LITTLE BOOK OF
AGA
TIPS
RICHARD MAGGS

THE LITTLE BOOK OF
CHRISTMAS
AGA
TIPS
RICHARD MAGGS

RAYBURN
THE LITTLE BOOK OF
RAYBURN
TIPS
RICHARD MAGGS

THE LITTLE BOOK OF
BRIDGE
TIPS

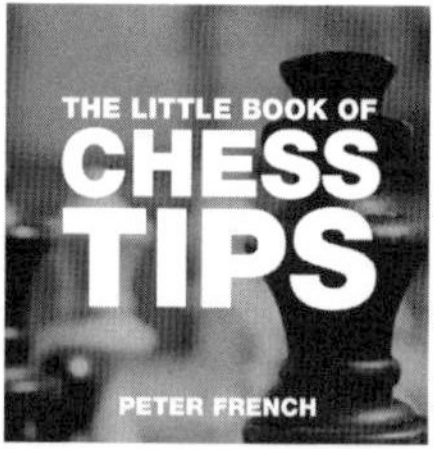
THE LITTLE BOOK OF
CHESS
TIPS
PETER FRENCH

THE LITTLE BOOK OF
FISHING
TIPS

THE LITTLE BOOK OF
GREEN
TIPS
WILLIAM FORTT

THE LITTLE BOOK OF
KITTEN
TIPS

MARMITE
PAUL HARTLEY
THE LITTLE BOOK OF
MARMITE
TIPS

THE LITTLE BOOK OF
PUPPY
TIPS
ANDREW LANGLEY

THE LITTLE BOOK OF
WHISKY
TIPS
ANDREW LANGLEY

THE LITTLE BOOK OF
TRAVEL
TIPS
MEGAN DEVENISH